SNOWMEN

1

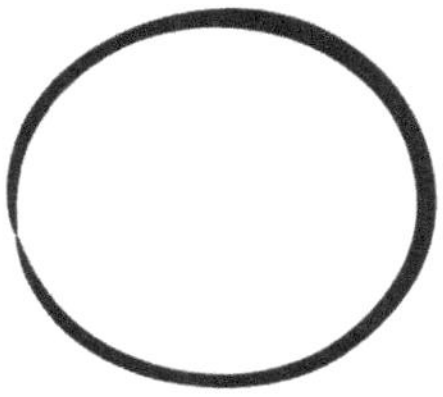

2

3

4

5

6

AIRPLANE

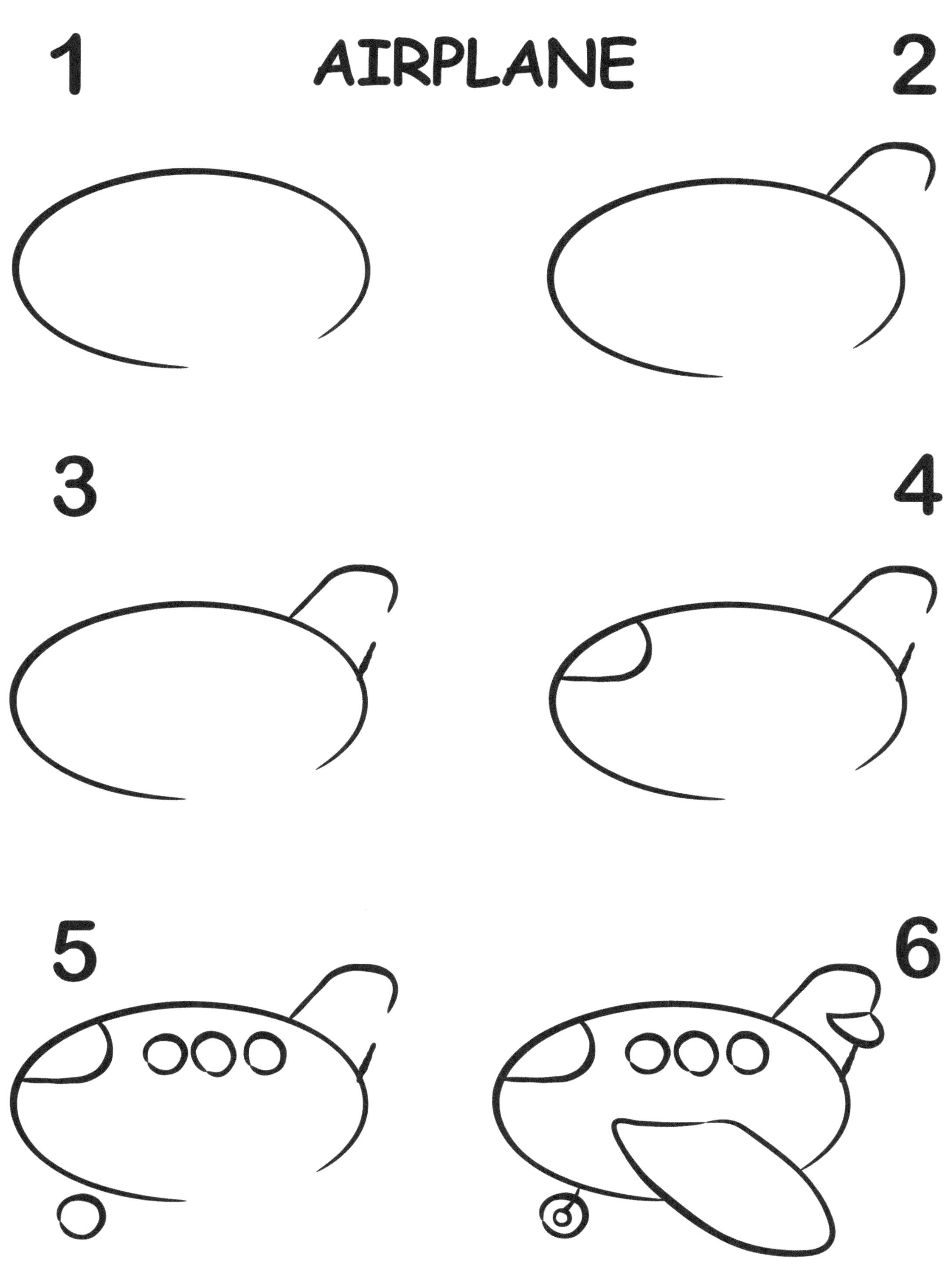

ASTRONAUT

1

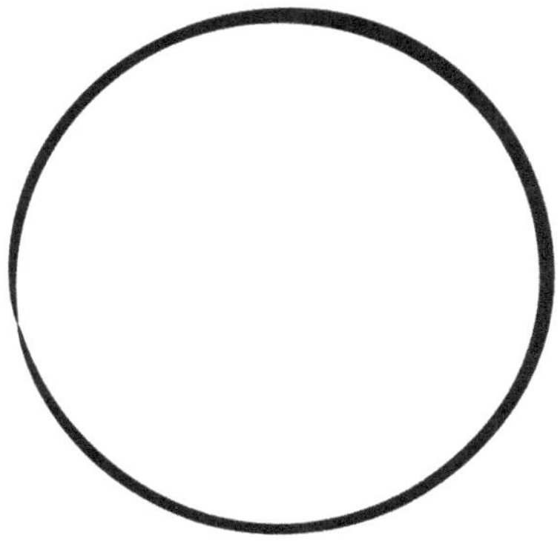

2

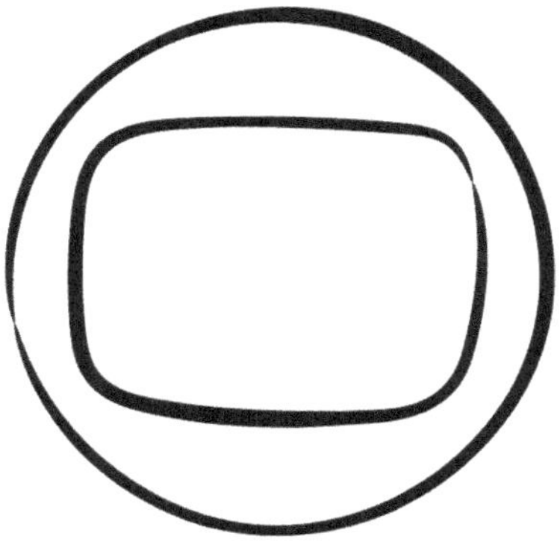

3

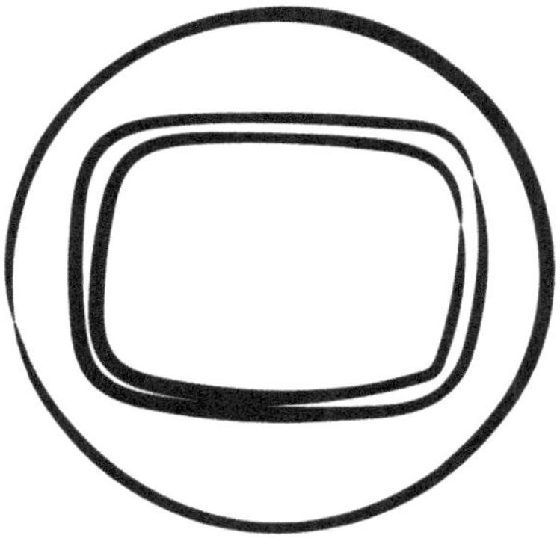

4

5

6

AIR BALOON

1

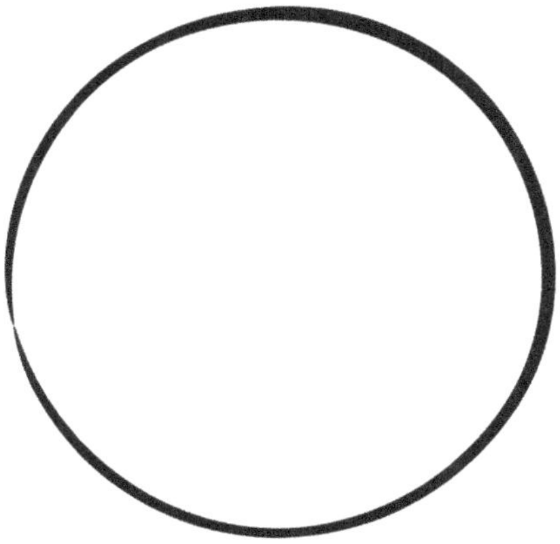

2

3

4

5

6

BEAR

1

2

3

4

5

6

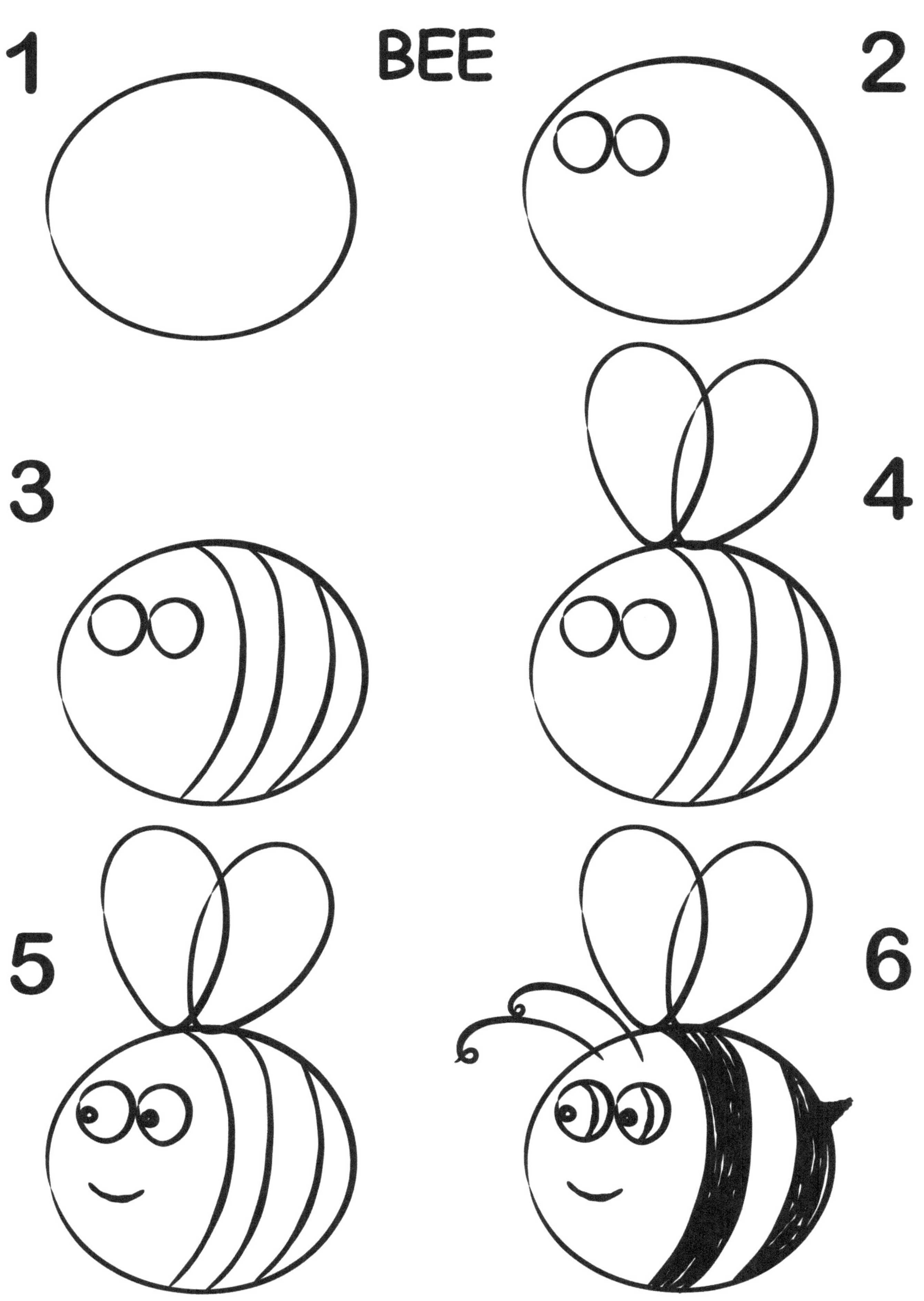

BEE
1
2
3
4
5
6

BICYCLE

1

2

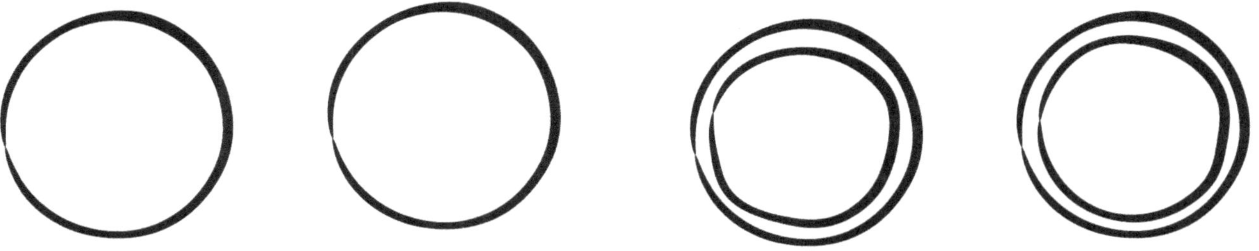

3

4

5

6

BOY

1

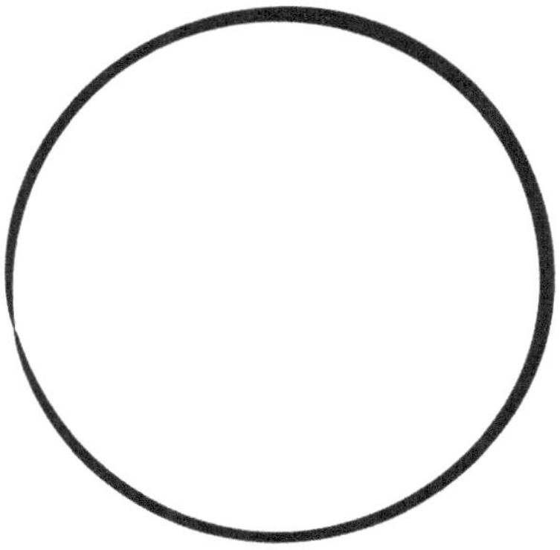

2

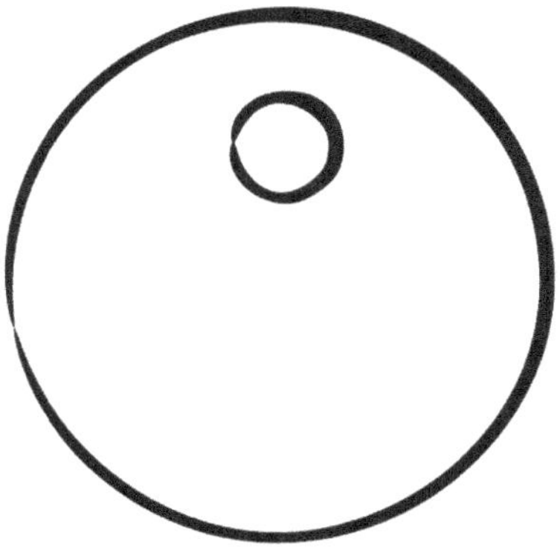

3

4

5

6

BULL

BUTTERFLY

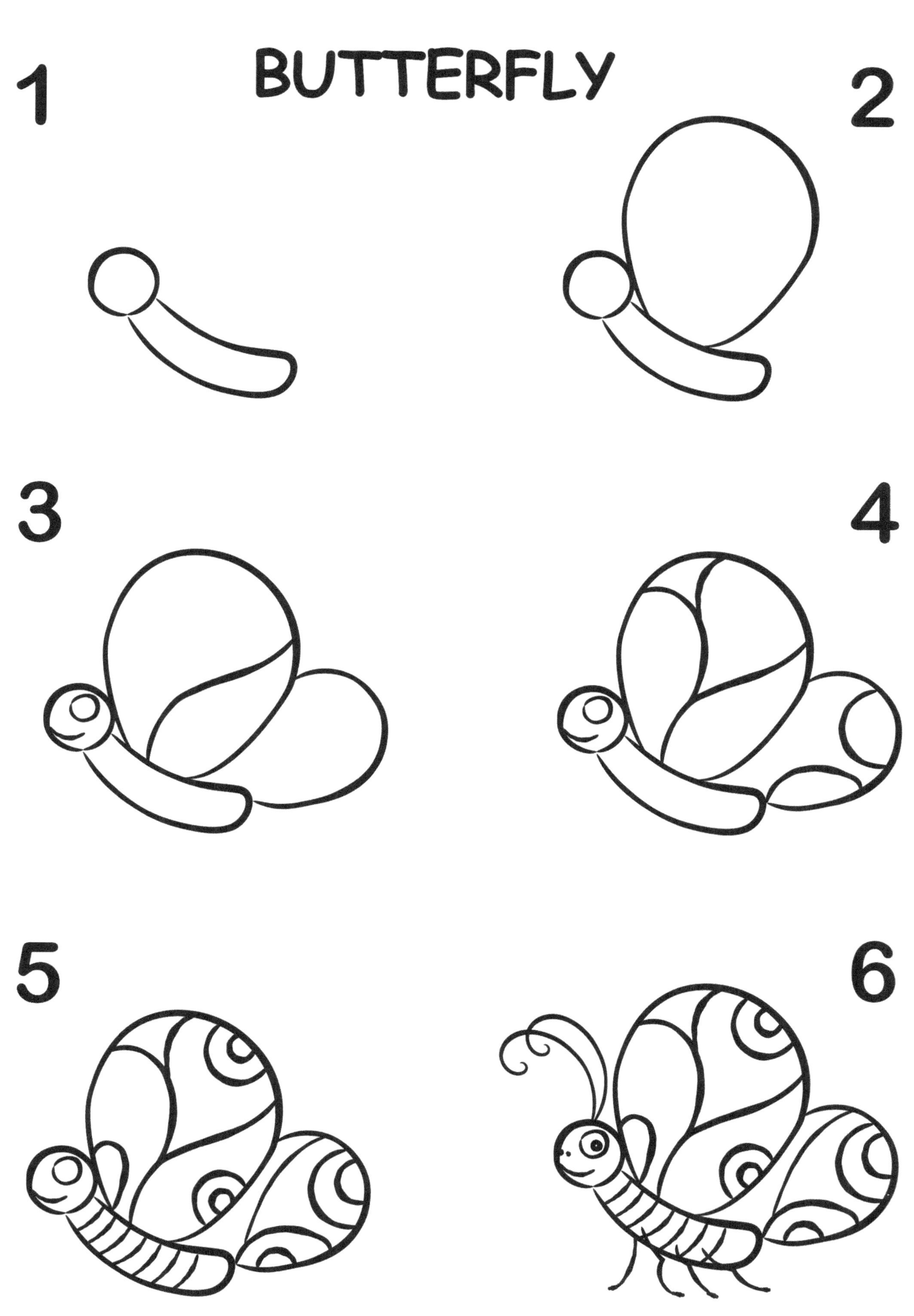

CAMERA

1

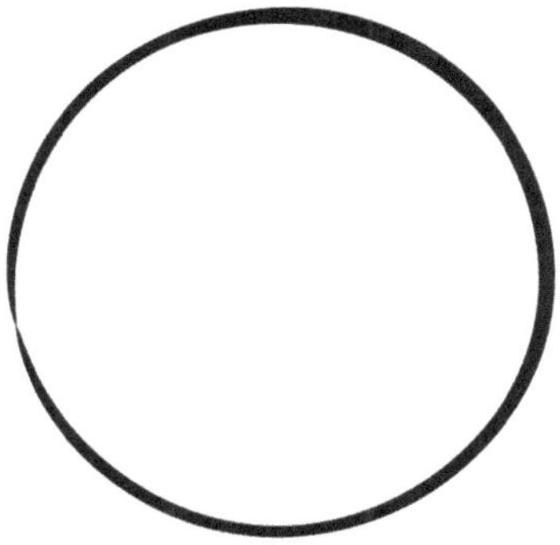

2

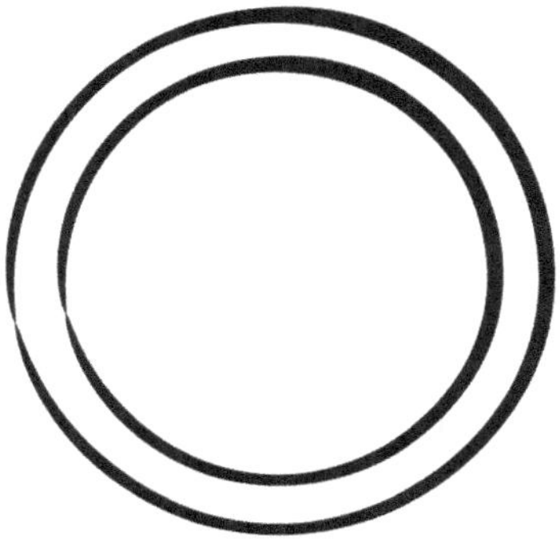

3

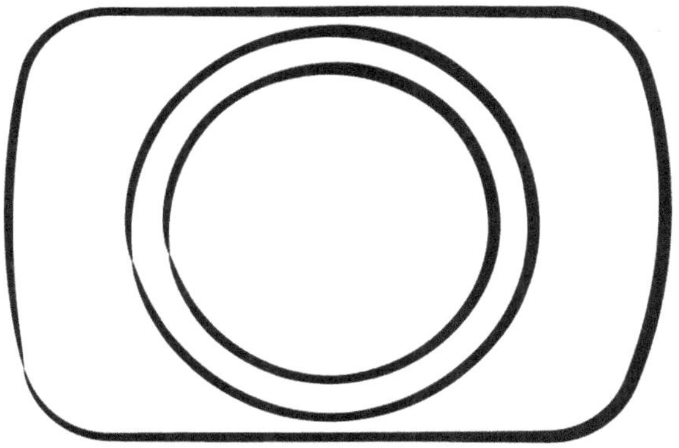

4

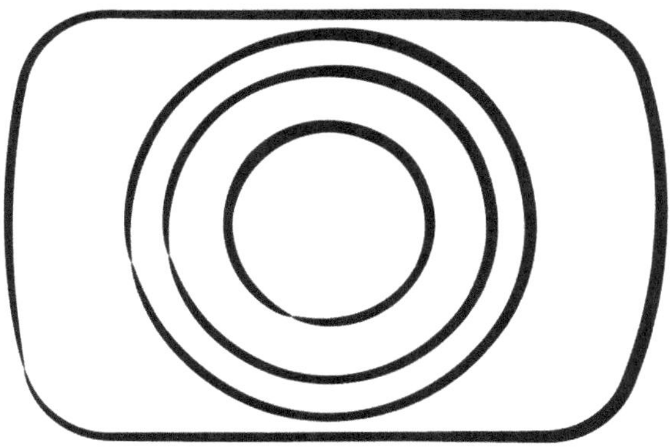

5

6

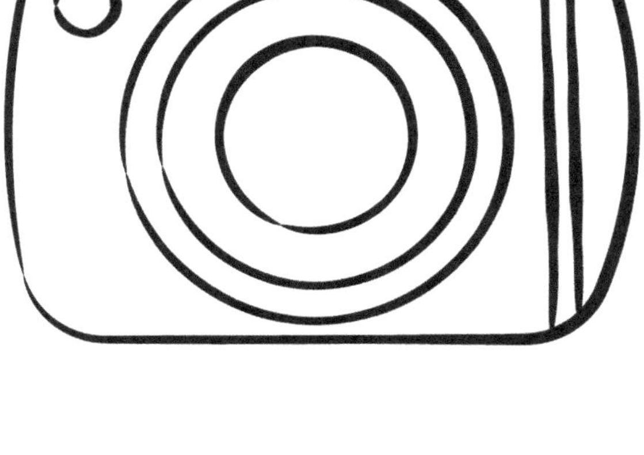

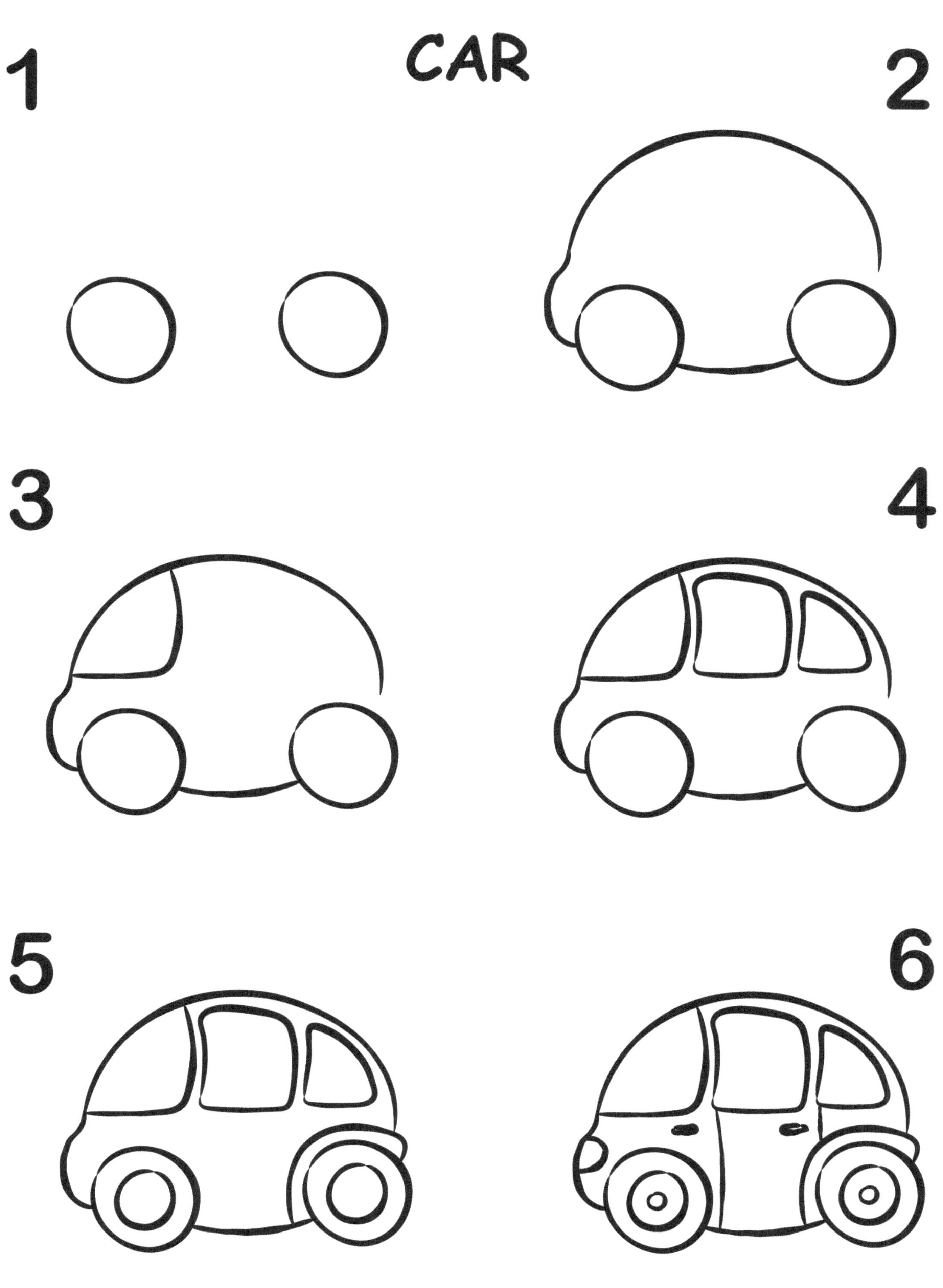

CAR
1
2
3
4
5
6

CAT

1

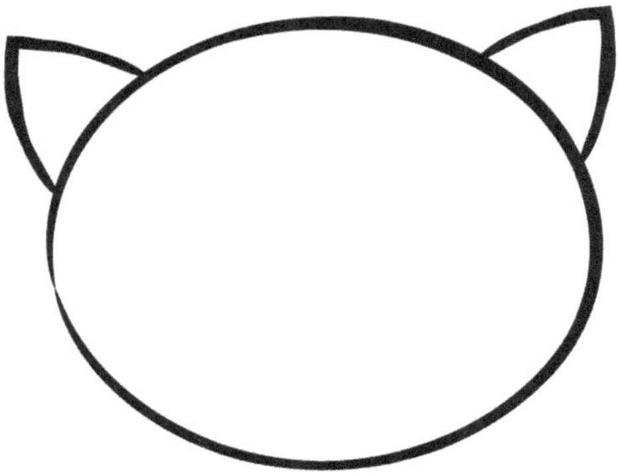

2

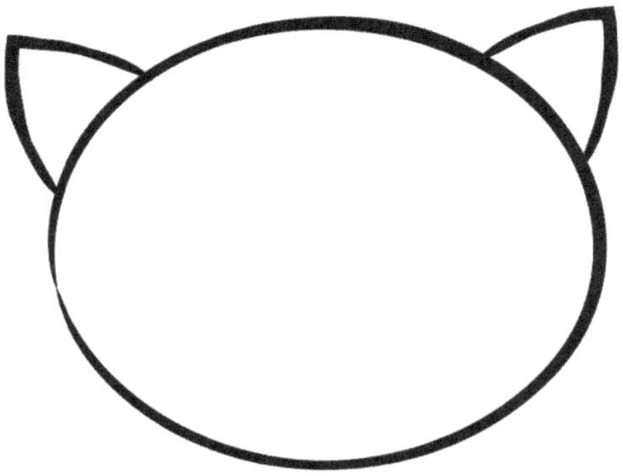

3

4

5

6

CHICKEN

1

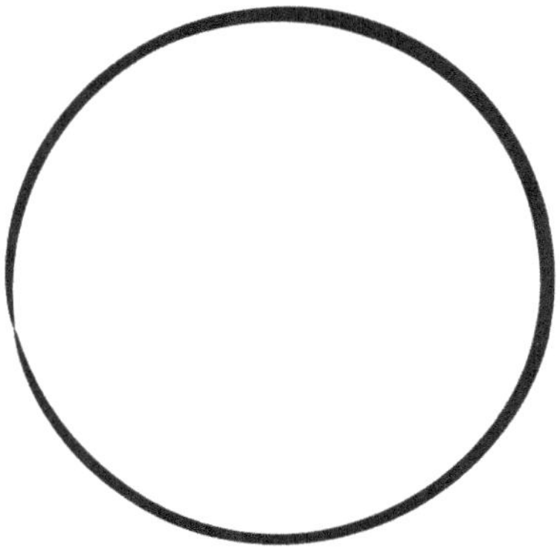

2

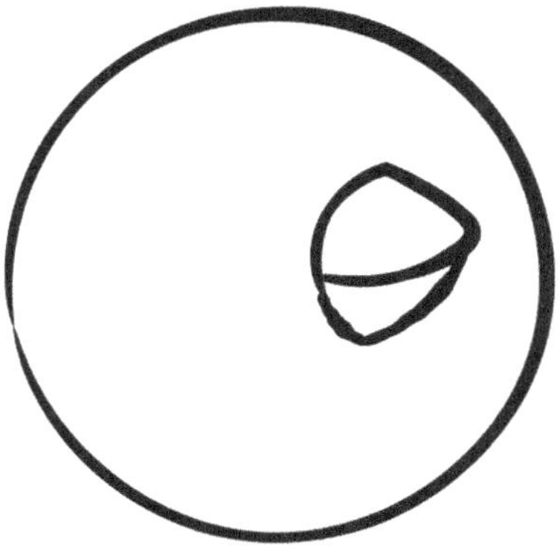

3

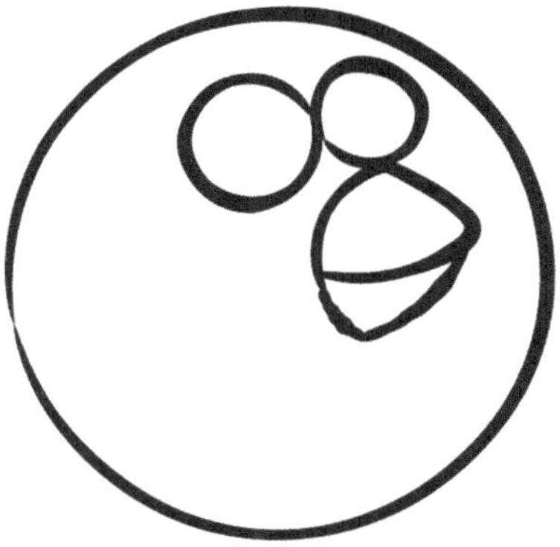

4

5

6

ALARM CLOCK

1

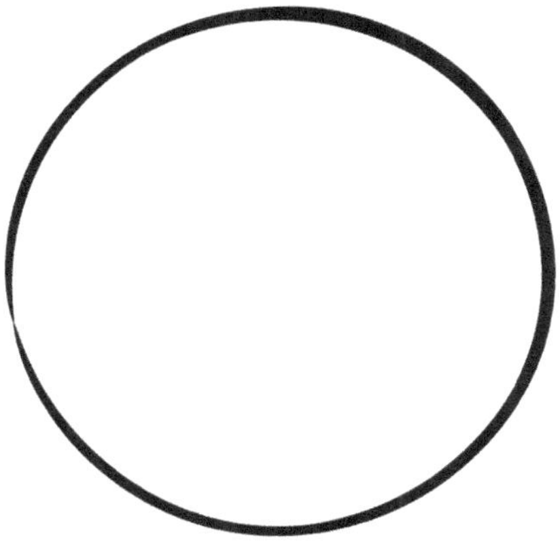

2

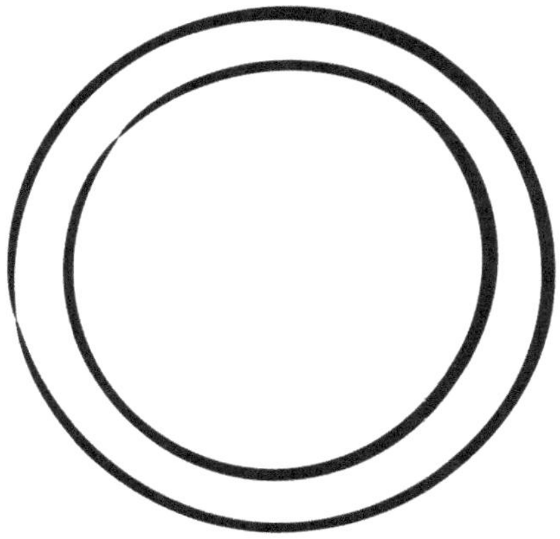

3

4

5

6

COW

1

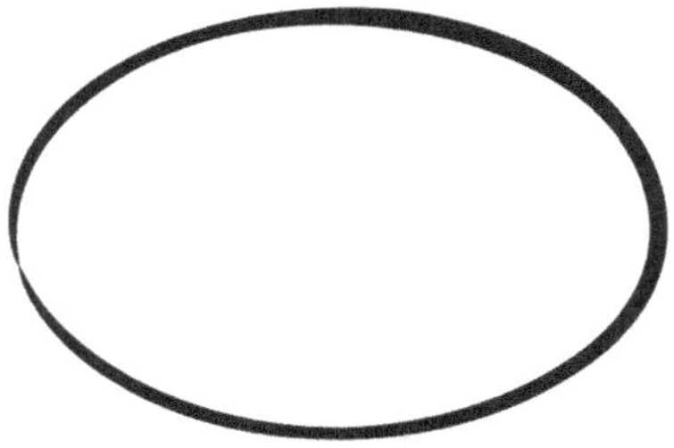

2

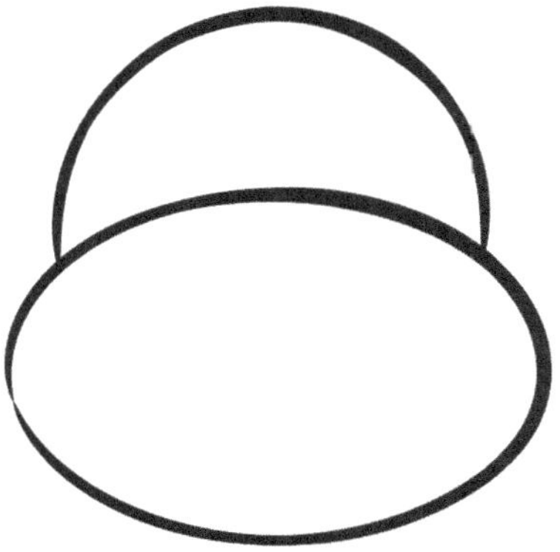

3

4

5

6

CRAB

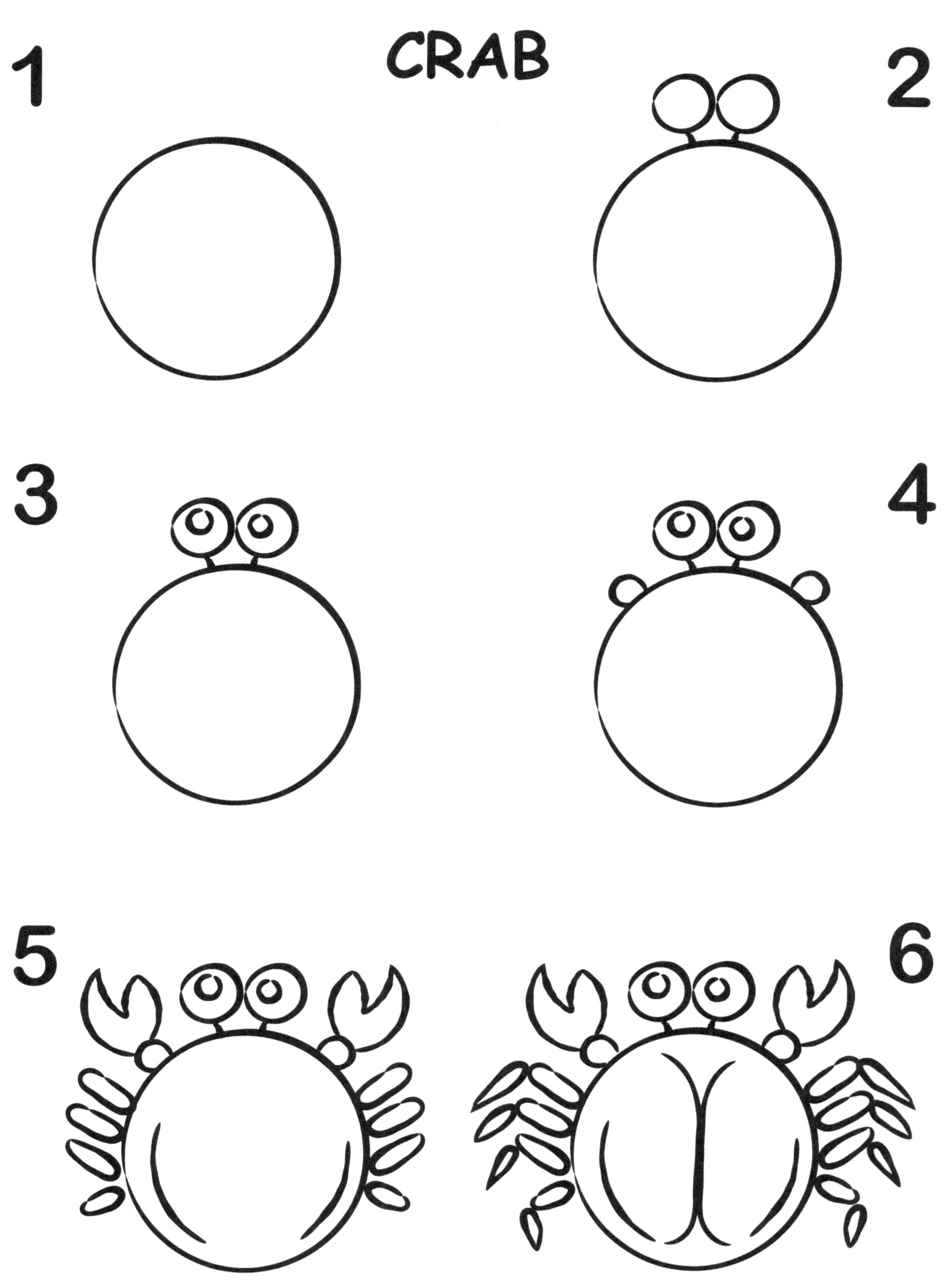

DEER

DOG

1

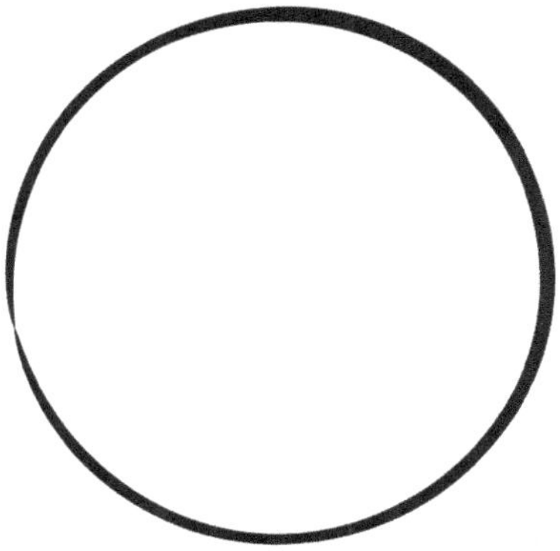

2

3

4

5

6

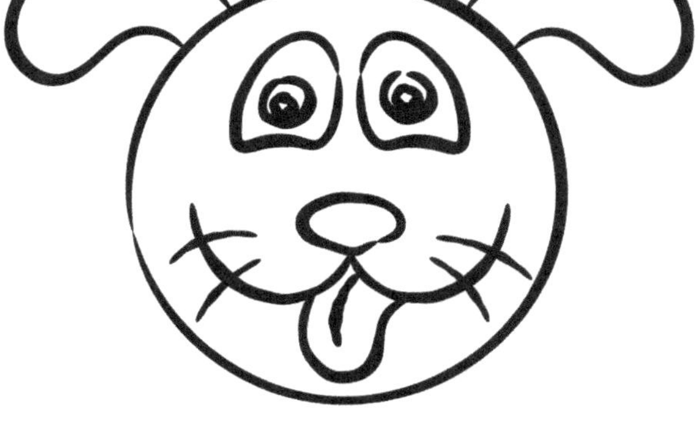

DOLPHIN

EAGLE

1

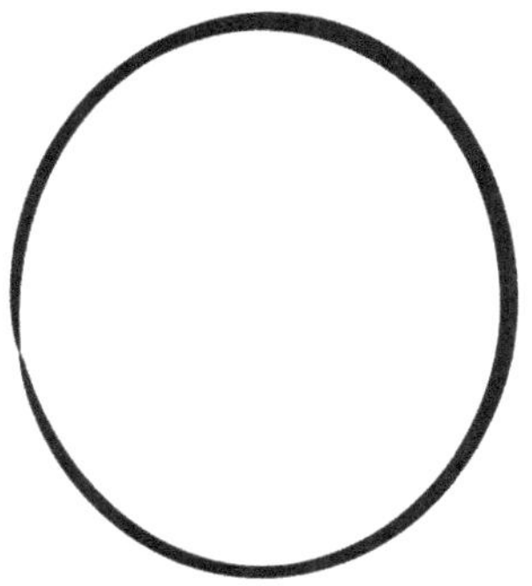

2

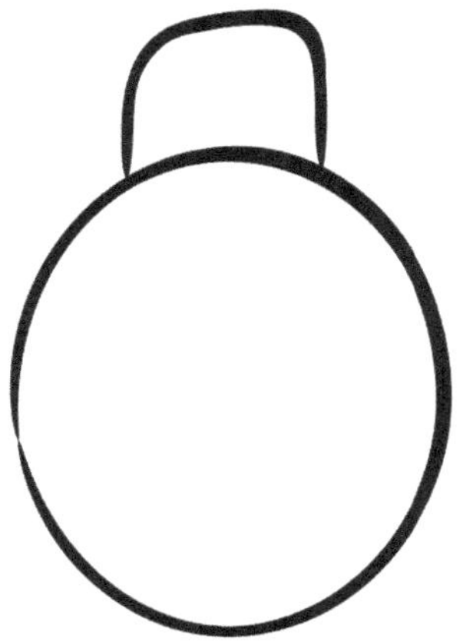

3

4

5

6

FISH

FLOWER

1

2

3

4

5

6

FROG

1

2

3

4

5

6

FLY

1

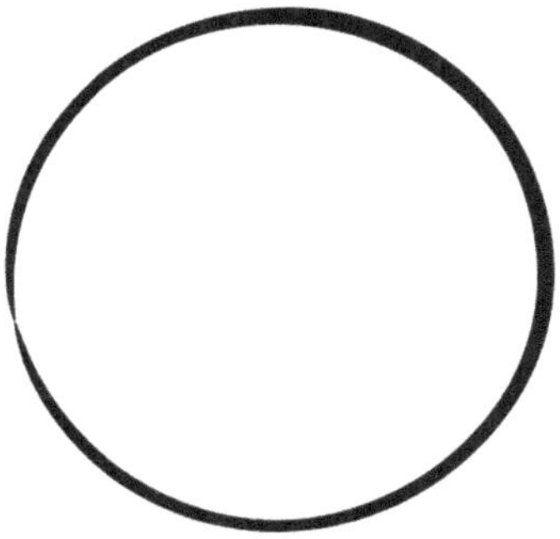

2

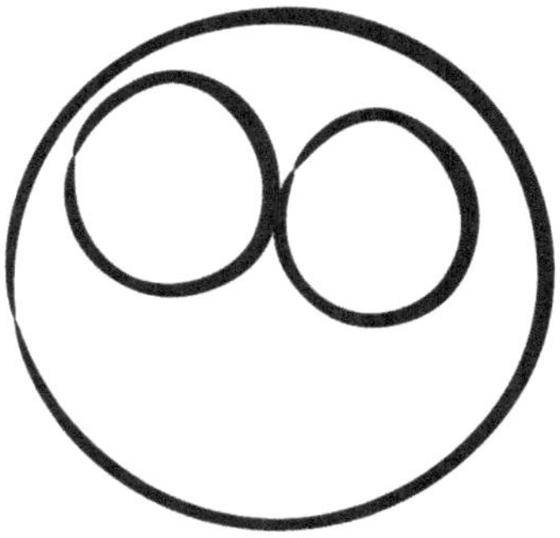

3

4

5

6

GINGERBREAD MEN

1

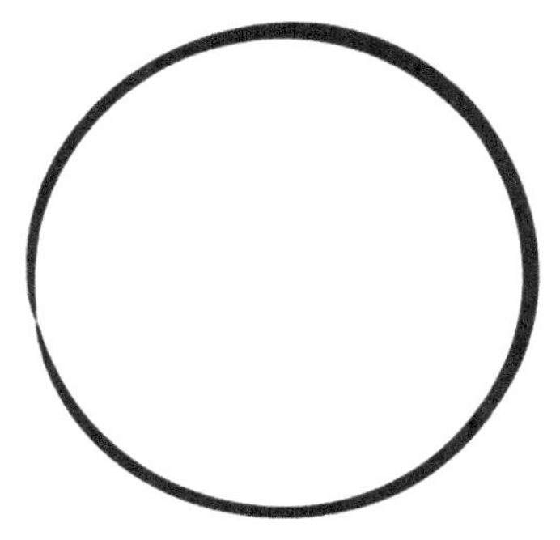

2

3

4

5

6

HELICOPTER

1

2

3

4

5

6

HORSE

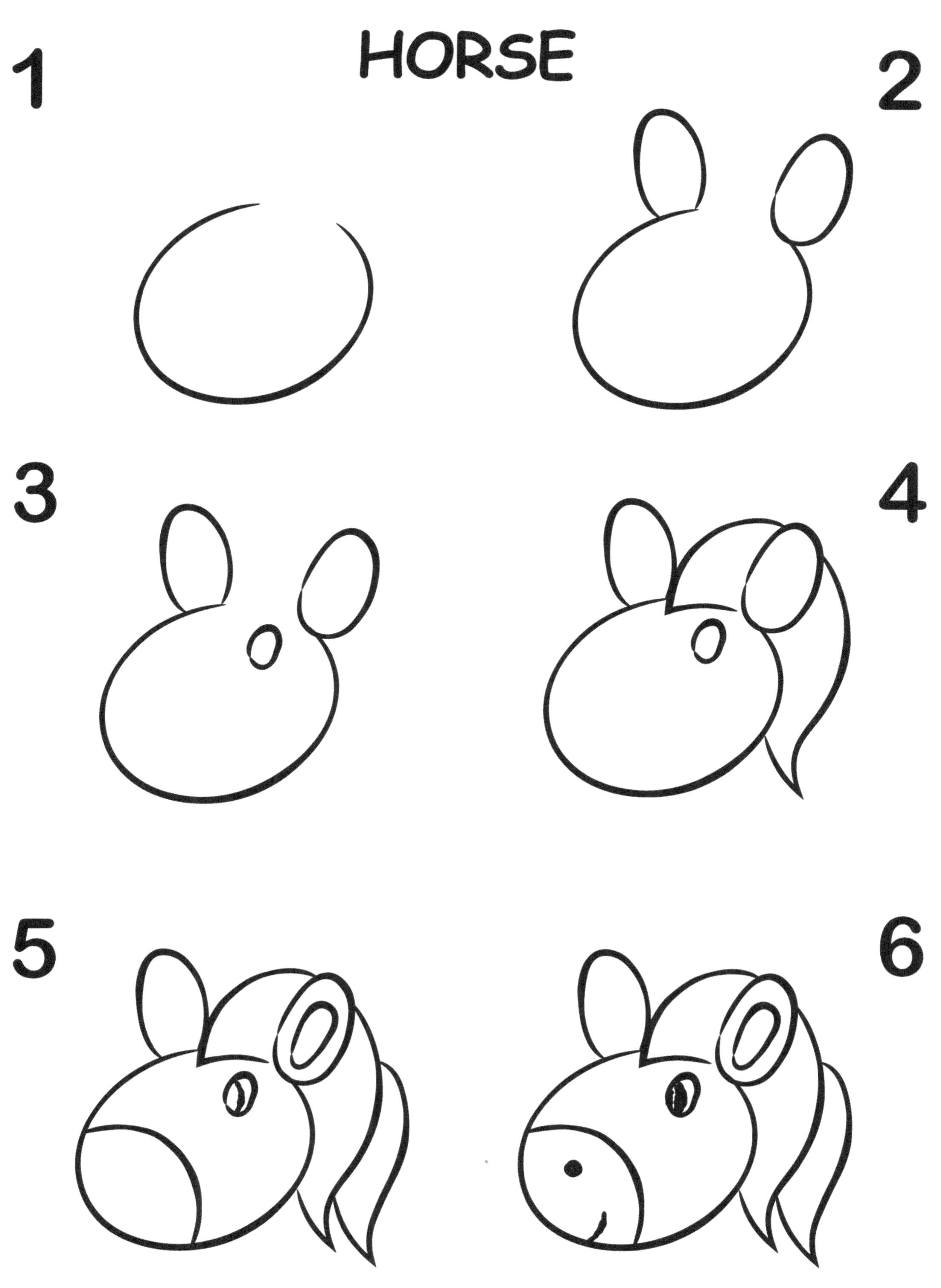

ICE CREAM

LADYBUG

1

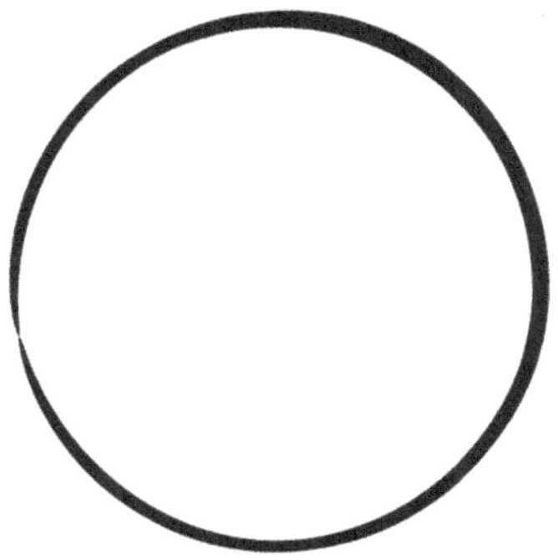

2

3

4

5

6

LION

MOUSE

1

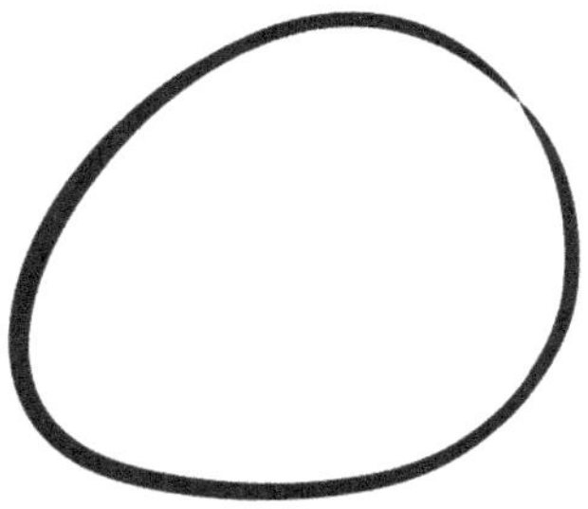

2

3

4

5

6

MONKEY

OWL

1

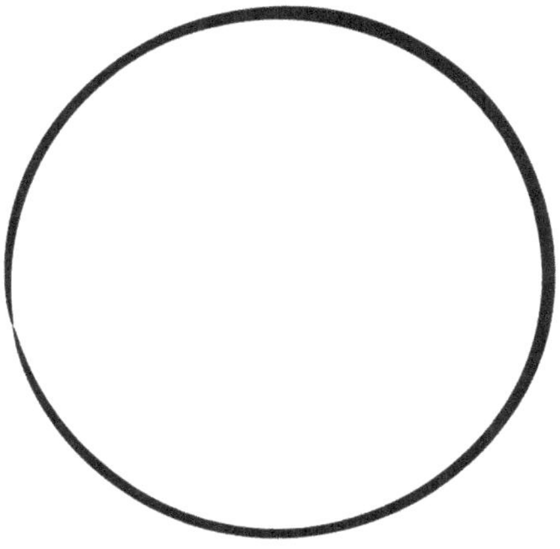

2

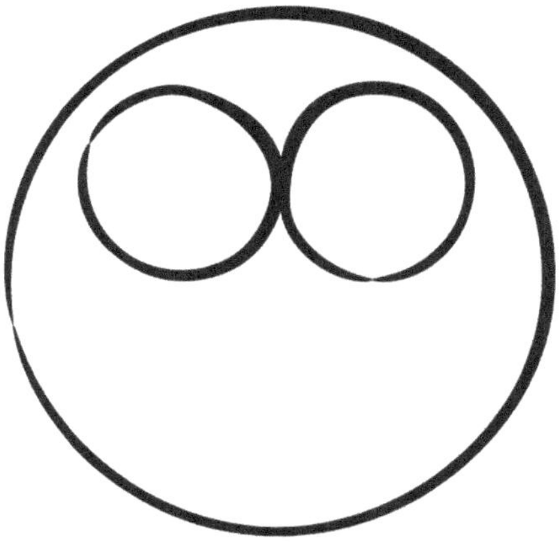

3

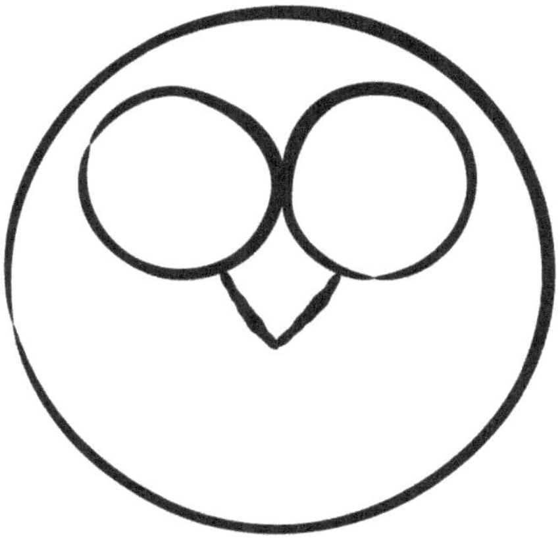

4

5

6

PANDA

HEDGEHOG

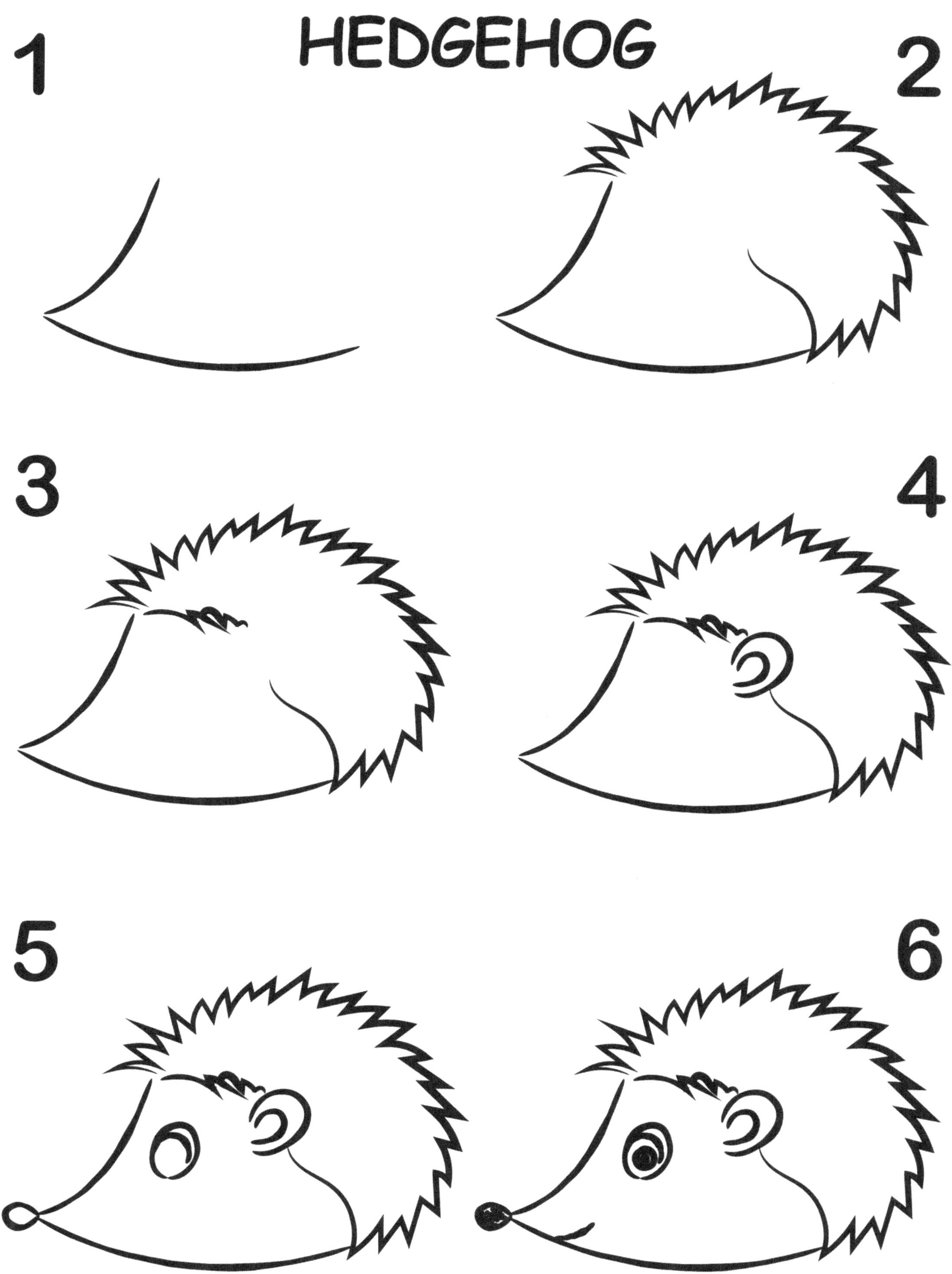

RABBIT

1

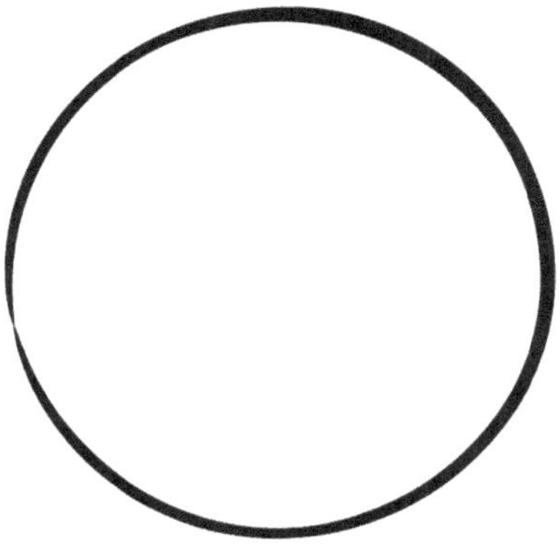

2

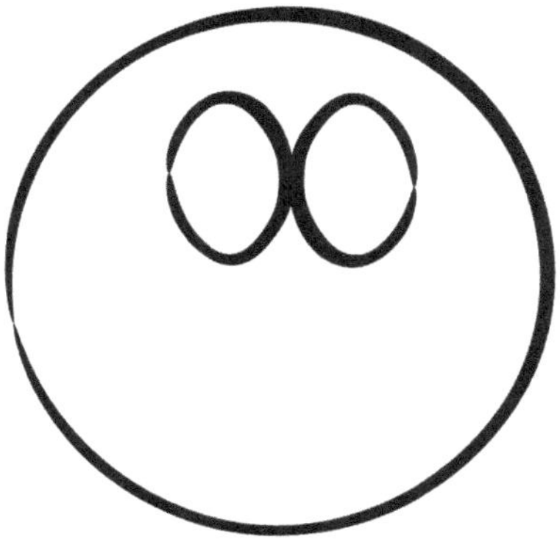

3

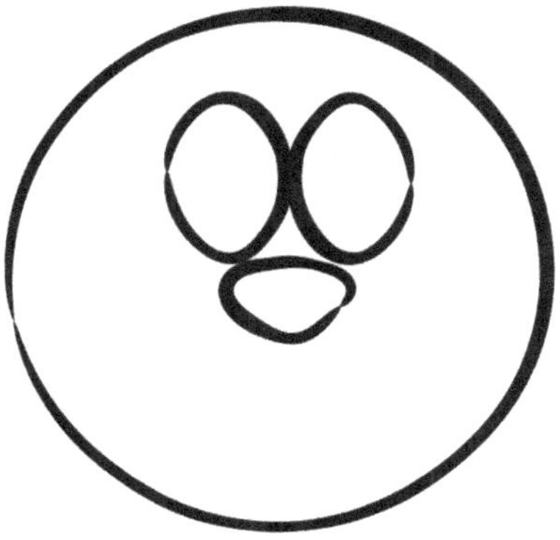

4

5

6

RACCOON

1

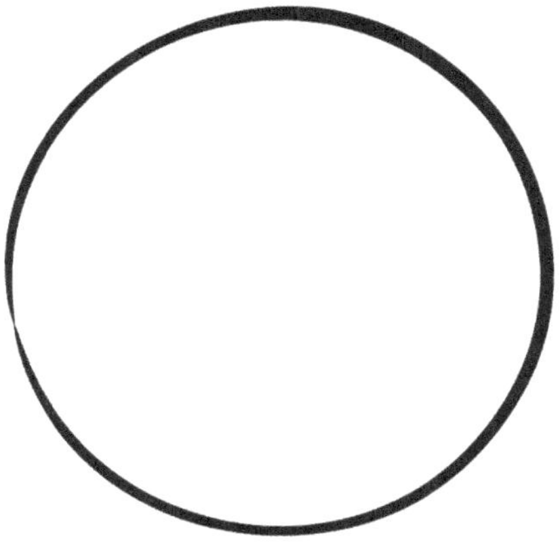

2

3

4

5

6

ROBOT

1

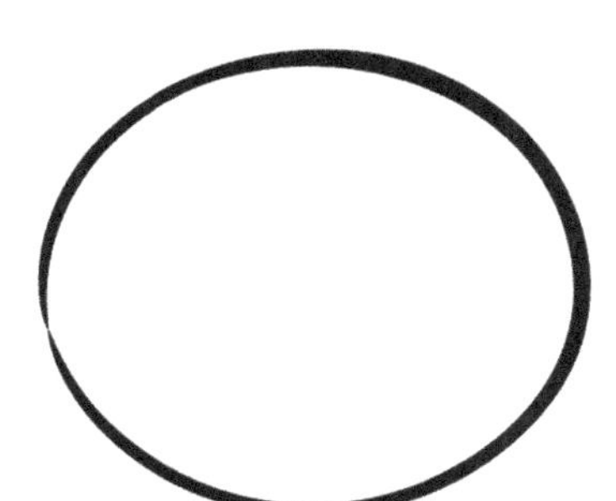

2

3

4

5

6

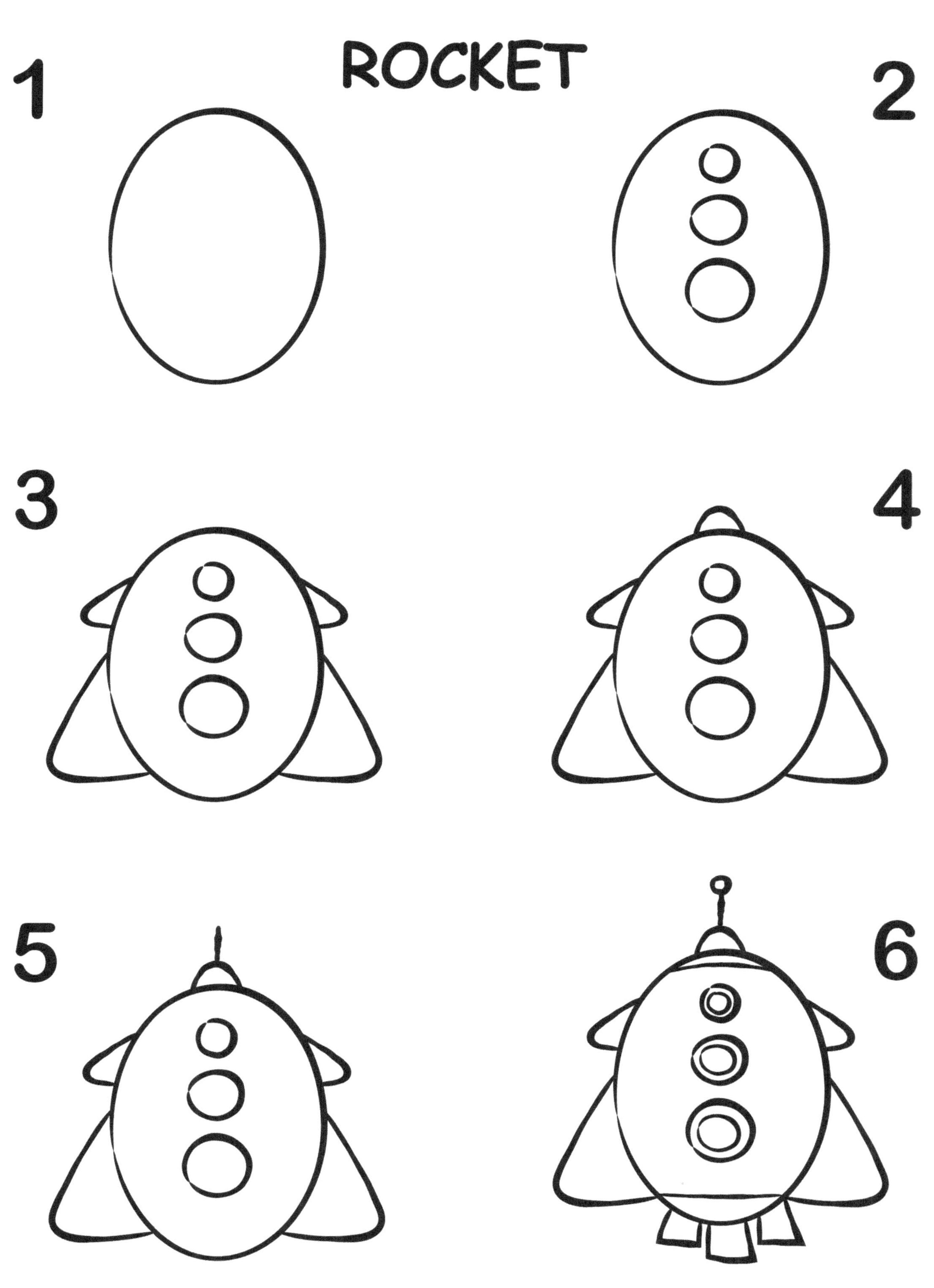

ROCKET
1
2
3
4
5
6

ROOSTER

1

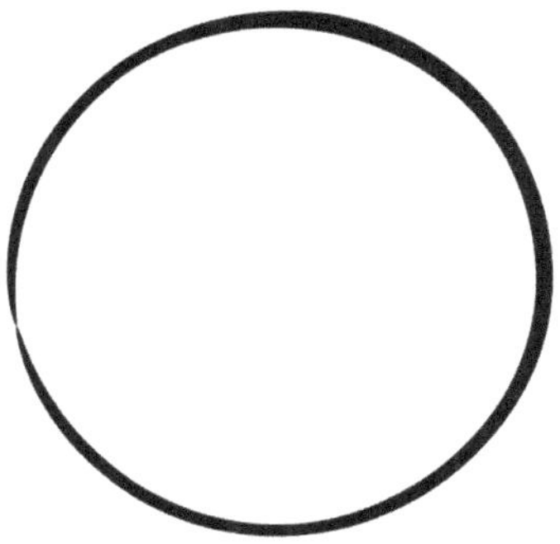

2

3

4

5

6

SEAHORSE

SNAIL

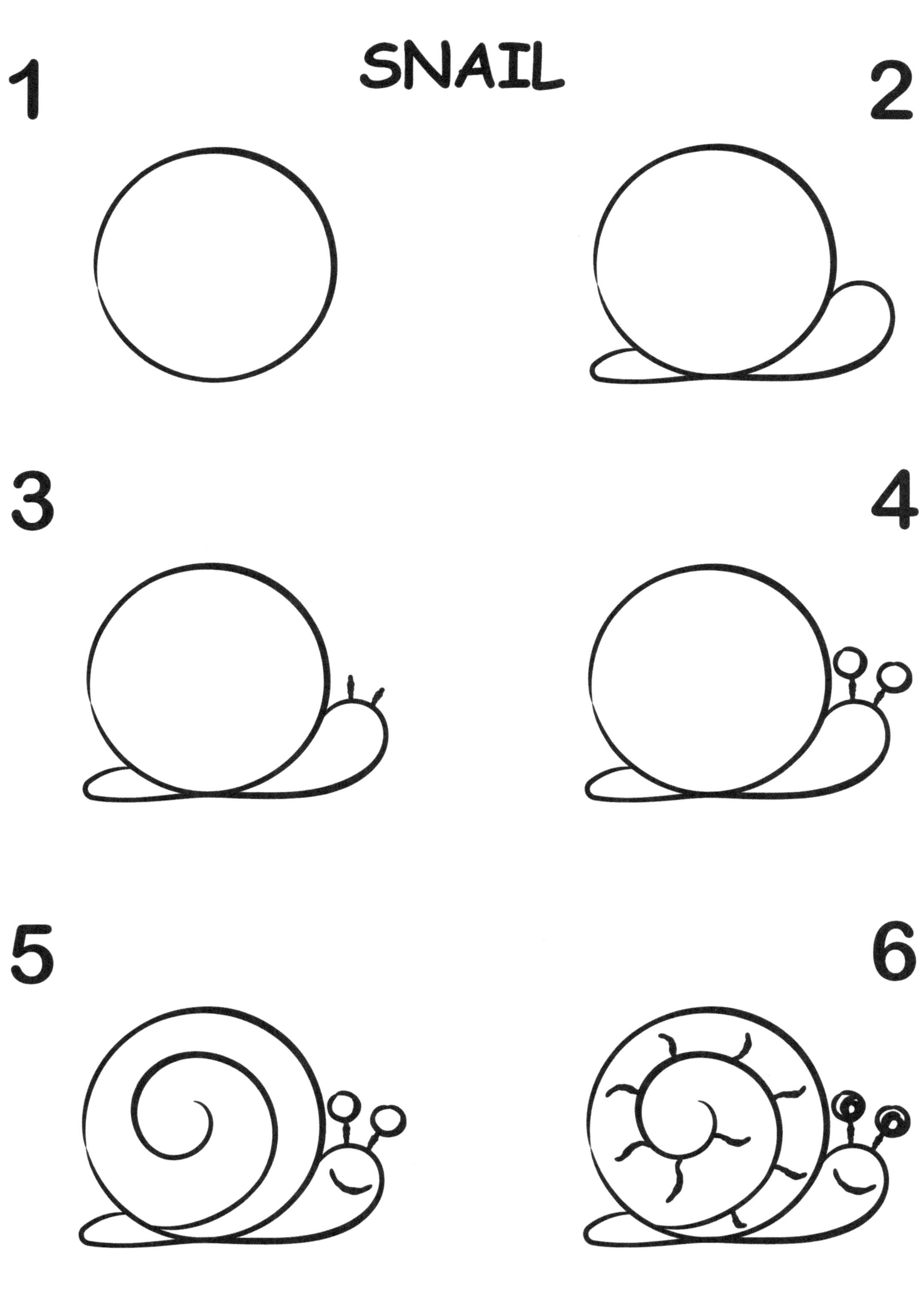

SPIDER

1

2

3

4

5

6

SQUIRREL

1

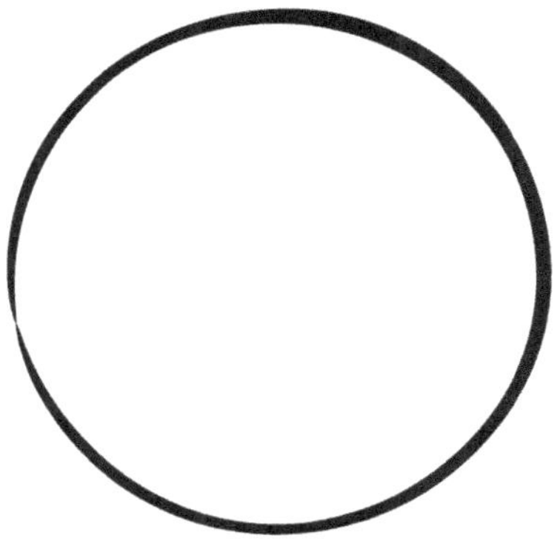

2

3

4

5

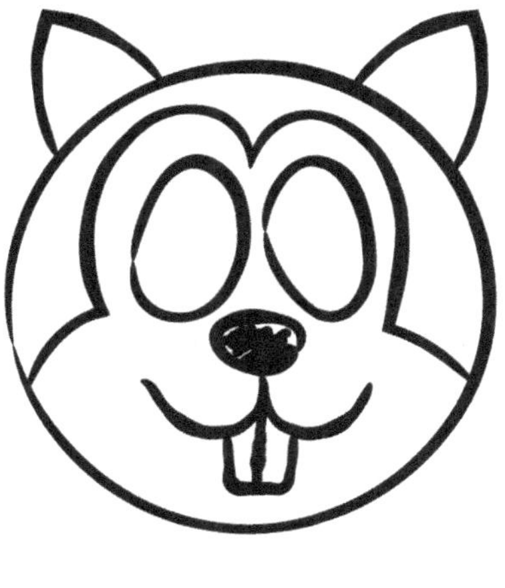

6

SUN

1

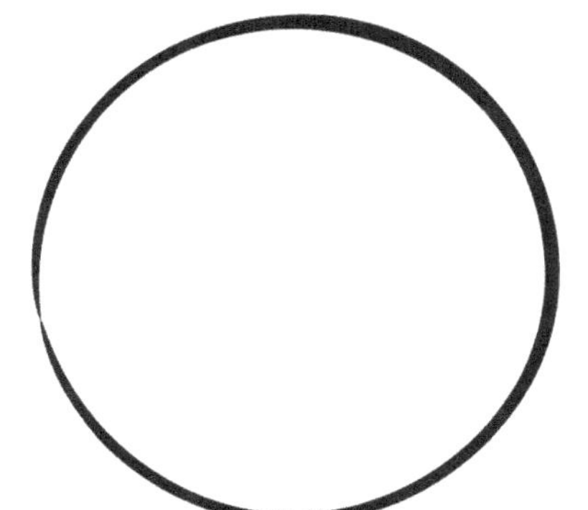

2

3

4

5

6

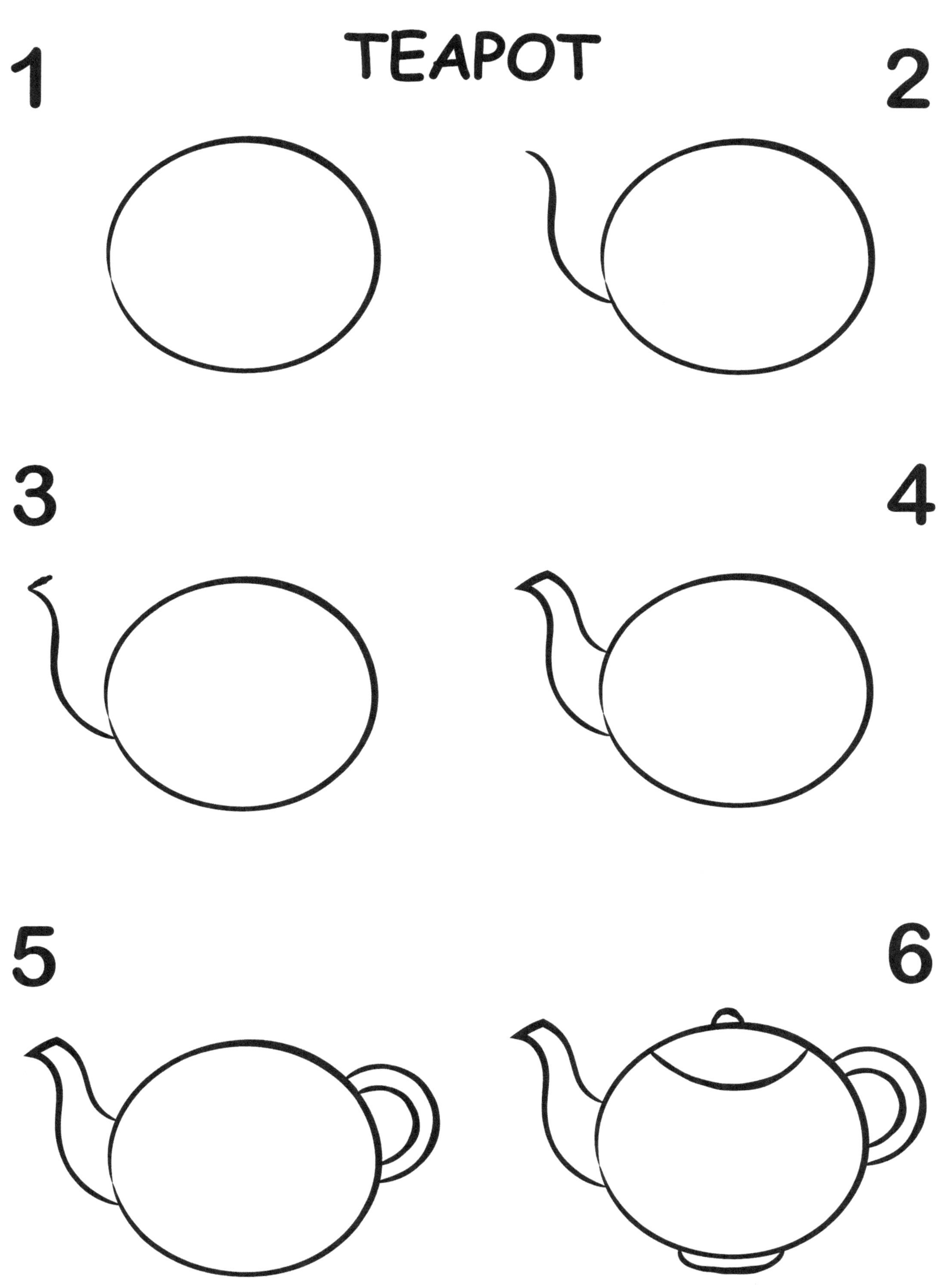

TEAPOT
1
2
3
4
5
6

TRAIN

1

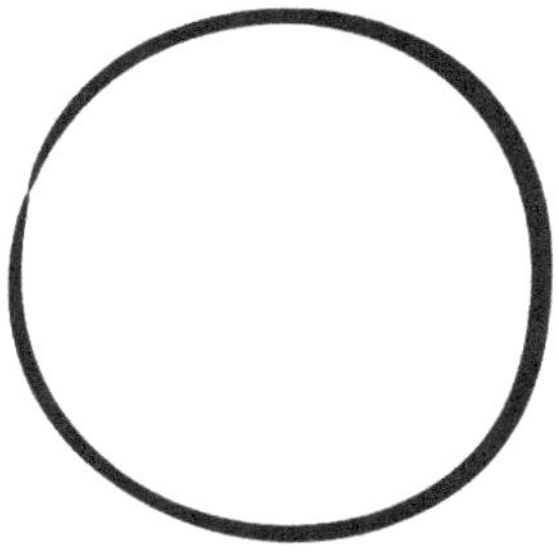

2

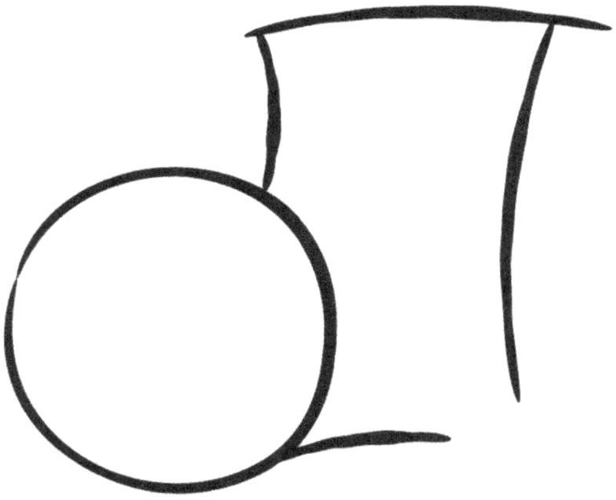

3

4

5

6

TURKEY

1

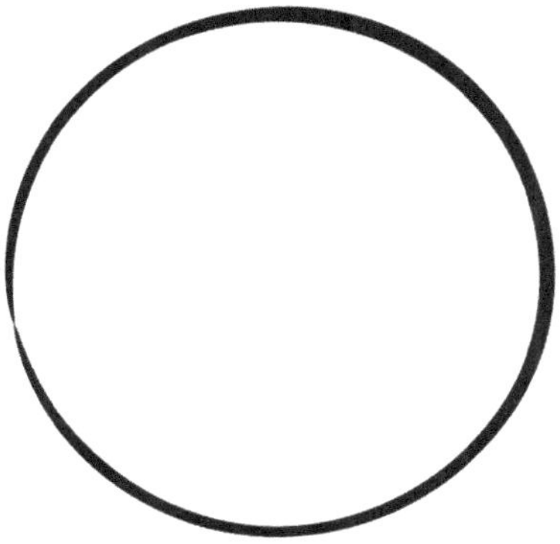

2

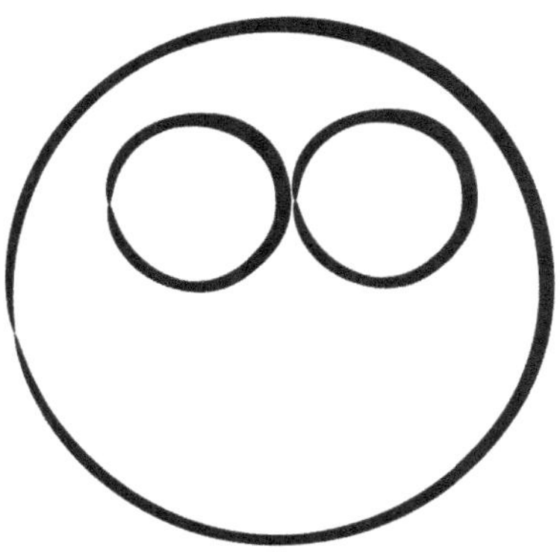

3

4

5

6

TURTLE

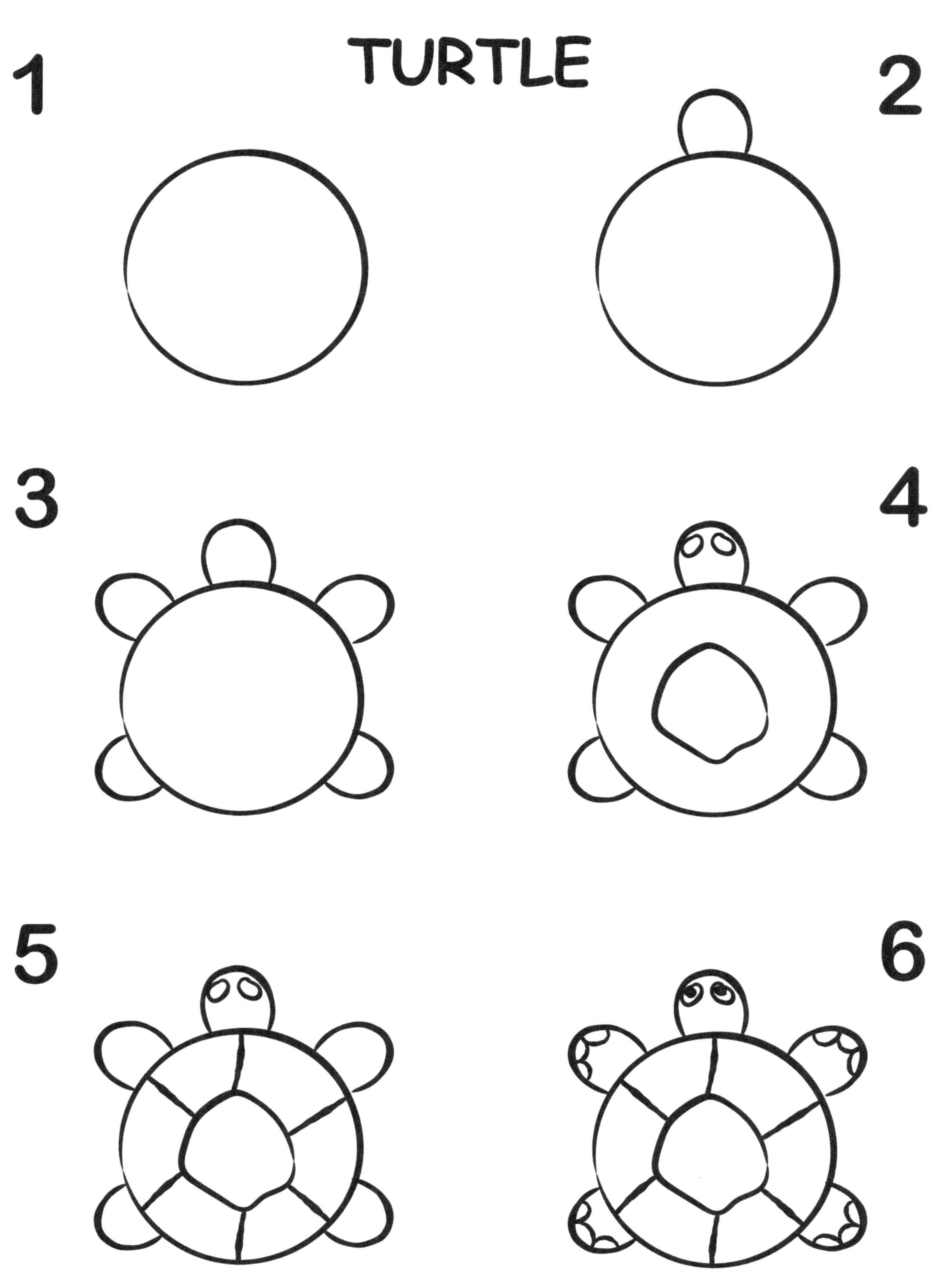